PLOT WRITING

STEP-BY-STEP

2 Manuscripts in 1 Book, Including:
Plotting and Story Structure

Sandy Marsh

More by Sandy Marsh

Discover all books from the Writing Best Seller Series by Sandy Marsh at:

bit.ly/sandy-marsh

Themed book bundles available at discounted prices:

bit.ly/sandy-marsh

Table of Contents

PLOTTING
STEP-BY-STEP

ESSENTIAL STORY PLOTTING, CONFLICT WRITING AND PLOTLINE TRICKS ANY WRITER CAN LEARN

SANDY MARSH

BOOK 1: PLOTTING

STEP-BY-STEP

Essential Story Plotting, Conflict Writing and Plotline Tricks Any Writer Can Learn

Sandy Marsh

reparation, damages, or monetary loss due to the information herein, either directly or indirectly.

Respective authors own all copyrights not held by the publisher.

The information herein is offered for informational purposes solely and is universal as so. The presentation of the information is without a contract or any type of guarantee assurance.

The trademarks that are used are without any consent, and the publication of the trademark is without permission or backing by the trademark owner. All trademarks and brands within this book are for clarifying purposes only and are the owned by the owners themselves, not affiliated with this document.

Table of Contents

Introduction

Thank you and congratulations for purchasing *"Plotting: Step-by-Step | Essential Story Plotting, Conflict Writing and Plotline Tricks Any Writer Can Learn"*.

In this book, we are going to further explore how you can write a rich plot that will not only give you plenty of material to write about but will also give you a depth of material that takes your story to the next level. The goal of designing a plotline is to establish a rich story that will intrigue your readers and give you, as the writer, the opportunity to have maximum impact on your storytelling process. Through creating a strong and productive plotline, you give yourself the power to take your story to greater heights and leave your readers with more to take away from the story itself in terms of lessons, experience, and entertainment.

Throughout this book, you are going to learn more about how you can write your own plot in such a way that will help you achieve those next-level results. You will learn about the basic structure of a plotline, as well as how you can build your own plot around this structure. Then, you will be guided through the process of taking your plot outline and bringing it to life in such a way that enables you to use this plotline for maximum impact. Finally, you will learn about some tips and tricks straight from the pros of story writing themselves. In this final chapter, you will be provided with everything you need to tie up any loose ends and make sure that you have a rock solid plotline that will drive your story forward in the most powerful, rewarding, and non-expecting ways possible.

If you are ready to learn how you can create the best plotline ever, and how you can execute it in your writing process so that it has maximum impact, then you are in the right place. Please take your time and build your plot alongside this book so that you can take in every piece of advice being offered and apply it to your own plot building practice. This will ensure that you are benefiting from all of the knowledge within' this book and that you have the best possible results. And of course, enjoy!

Chapter 1: A Basic Plot Outline

Plot outlines, like with story outlines and story structures, have a specific sequence that they are usually created in. While you can choose to alter the timing of this sequence, it is always best that you stick to the sequence itself. This will ensure that you are using the proper and best outline available to help you create a rich and powerful plot. In this chapter, you are going to explore what this basic outline is, as well as every element that exists in this outline. You will also gain an understanding as to why the structure is built this way, and how this contributes to your successful story plot. By the end, you should have a strong understanding as to how this structure works, why it works, and how it looks in stories when it has been executed effectively.

What is the Purpose of The Plot Outline?

Like with all of the elements of your story that we have discussed until now, the plot outline or plot diagram has a very profound and powerful purpose when it comes to your story writing process and experience. This tool is specifically used to help you choose major plot points and organize them along a story arc so that you can identify what your story will be like beforehand. The reason you do this is for several reasons, though it is primarily for the purpose of organizing your plot sequencing so that the story pans out in a strong, chronological manner that allows it to flow efficiently and effectively.

Many people believe that using something such as a plot outline will restrict the writing process and prevent them from having creative freedom and expression when it comes to writing the novel. There are many ways to help further open up the opportunity for creative expression, but ultimately this is not the case. Having a plot outline does not need to mean that you specifically plan out each minor element of your book before you get to the writing process. Instead, it gives you the opportunity to get an overall idea of where you are going with your novel and how you can get there while providing and delivering the best story possible. This is more about embracing your creative freedom and using it to guide you towards a story that leaves a massive impact on your readers than it is about eliminating your creative freedom and forcing you to think about all of the details *right now* rather than as they come to you.

Plot outlines serve as a great backbone to your story. These provide the bare bone basics of your story, what you want to include in it, and how you want to deliver it to your readers. As you are writing, you still have the power to switch things around, including enormous amounts of creativity in the actual writing process, and otherwise, add your own personal touch to your novel. Having the plot outline simply means that you know what general direction to head in and when and where things should happen within' your book so that you are capable of delivering a strong story that has the ability to engage, impress, and excite your readers, no matter what genre you are writing in.

What the Outline Looks Like

The outline looks somewhat like an unfinished triangle or the moving chart that gathers information on a person's heartbeat.

It starts out as a flat line, spikes up to create a triangular shape, and then comes back down to the flat line. This is the most basic plot outline that exists, and it is the one that virtually every story follows. Although you may slightly alter where the spike exists on your own diagram, or how much rising action and falling action exist before and after the spike, the shape remains generally untouched, and it serves as an excellent representation of what your plot outline should look like. Because of the shape of this spike, it is also known as a story arc.

Where the plotline starts, with the flatline, is known as an exposition. This is the beginning of your novel, and it serves by providing you with the opportunity to introduce your characters and the other important elements of the book. This is where you want to introduce the setting of your novel, the stakes that your character(s) are concerned about, and what the problem is. It is through this that you gain the momentum within your novel that will allow you to accelerate towards the problem while keeping your reader engaged, as here is where you give them a reason to care and have the interest to keep reading what you have written.

Once you have successfully completed the exposition, you want to introduce the rising action. This is the part of the story where you practice suspense-building techniques to keep your reader engaged and involved. You are using this part of the book to climb towards the climax of the story. Here, the problem that your character(s) are facing is getting worse, and the complications are exceeding. Usually, this rising action takes course over many pages and even chapters so that you can generate a large element of suspense before you eventually arrive at the climax. Here, you can introduce problems and solve them all well before reaching the actual climax. The primary purpose is to draw the story up to where "it" happens, with "it" being the big reason why you are telling the story in the first place.

The climax is usually around the middle of the story, though it can take place sooner or later depending on how you have chosen to write the story and where you have introduced each unique plot element. This is the most exciting and typically most rewarding part of the story, especially for readers, because it gives them satisfaction after all of the rising action you have shared with them until now. This is the part that makes the reader question "what's next?" and want to keep reading to find out.

Once you have worked through the climax of your story, you officially fall into a decline otherwise known as falling action. This is where the "what now?" part of the climax is revealed as you give your reader an idea of what the resolution is following the climax of your story. You use this as an opportunity to tie up loose ends, to explain where things go after the climax, and to give your reader an opportunity to reflect on the rest of the story. You answer any questions that may have been left behind throughout the rest of the story and generally work towards closing *most* things off in this area. This is where you are working towards the resolution.

The end of the story is also known as the resolution, and this is where the resolution is actually identified. You use this part of the book to inform your reader as to how the resolution has affected each character, how things have turned out for them, and where they are now that the story's problem has been resolved. You close up all of the final loose ends here and provide answers to any unanswered questions. This is where you ultimately provide closure for your book, your characters, and your reader.

Following this plot outline or diagram gives you the opportunity to use a story arc that works. Virtually every story is built along this diagram in one way or another. Sometimes the climax takes place sooner or later than the center of the story, but this is typically how books are written. This outline is used because it works, but also because it gives you a structured outline to help you write the information that your readers need in order for the story to have a positive impact on them. Using this story arc or plot diagram gives you the opportunity to have plenty of time to introduce different elements of the story and explain them in enough detail that your reader has time to collect all of the information they need to experience the story in a powerful manner.

Examples of Plot Outlines

There are many examples of plot outlines available to you, especially if you are an avid reader, television or movie watcher, or story listener. Virtually every story you have ever heard follows this structure in one way or another. However, to give you a few easy ideas of how this outline looks when it is in practice, let's look at two unique stories: The Three Little Pigs and Cinderella.

In three little pigs, we are introduced through the exposition where the three pigs are moving away from their family home, and each is in search of a new home. We are presented with who they are, what they are doing, and why. We are also given an idea of what is at stake for them: their homes. It moves forward into the rising action when we learn about each of the pigs looking for building materials and then building their homes. We learn that one builds theirs out of a weaker material (straw), one builds theirs out of a stronger material (twigs), and one builds theirs out of the strongest material (bricks). We are informed about the varying strengths of these materials, giving us the idea that there is some importance behind this piece of information but not yet introducing why. The story continues to rise as we later are introduced to the big bad wolf who comes along and huffs and puffs to blow down the first house which is made of straw. As you likely already know, the house blows down right away, and the pig runs off to his brother's house, which is made of twigs. The big bad wolf then goes and blows down the twig house and huffs and puffs and blows down that house as well. So, the two pigs are left running away to their other brother's house, which is made of bricks. There, the pigs are safe from the big bad wolf's huffing and puffing. The climax of the story arrives when the wolf finds a way to climb onto the roof of the house and comes down the chimney. There, he falls into a pot of boiling water, and the pigs cook him up. The falling action is that the pigs enjoy a feast together and are free of their fear of being eaten up by the big bad wolf. The resolution is that the three pigs end up sharing the home together and living with each other "happily ever after."

Cinderella is another popular fairy tale which also introduces us to what a plot diagram looks like in action. Here, the exposition lies within' Cinderella being introduced to the readers. We learn that she is a step-child and that her dad is no longer around, so she lives with her evil step-mom and two evil step-sisters. The step-mom and step-sisters live selfish lives of happiness and joy whilst forcing Cinderella to take care of the household by overseeing the chores and ensuring that it is well looked after. The rising action is when Cinderella overhears about an upcoming ball and insists that she wants to go. The step-mom says she can only go if all of her work is complete, and then ensures that there is so much work to be done that Cinderella will never be done in time. A fairy godmother comes and grants Cinderella her wish of going to the ball. She even ensures that Cinderella has a beautiful outfit and that she is cleaned up nicely for the experience so that she isn't late and all she has to do is get there. The climax arrives when Cinderella is at the ball. There, the prince falls in love with her and insists that they get married. When she realizes that the clock is about to strike midnight, she runs out without leaving her name or any contact information with the prince. However, she does lose a glass slipper on her way out of the ball. The falling action starts when the prince picks up the shoe and insists that he and his servants find Cinderella. They take the glass slipper and visit every house in the land to find the lady whom the glass slipper belongs to. Cinderella is almost robbed of the opportunity to try on the glass slipper when her step-mother tries to lock her in the basement, but she manages to get out. The resolution is finally granted to us when we learn that the glass slipper fits her perfectly and she is, in fact, the lady that the prince wanted to marry the night before. The step-mom is furious and so are the step-sisters as they learn that they are not the one who gets to marry the prince. Cinderella, on the other hand, is granted the opportunity to marry the prince, and she is freed from her life as a servant for her ungrateful and evil step-mom and step-sisters.

As you can see in both of these stories, there are very clear expositions, rising actions, climaxes, falling actions, and resolutions. These are the primary requirements of a story to keep it moving so that readers remain engaged and curious about how the story ends. Without these primary elements, the story may become stagnant, fail to draw readers through a chronological series of events that flow effectively through the storyline or otherwise deliver the story in such a way that helps us stay invested in it and curious as to what the resolution will be. Ultimately, the entire purpose of these plot diagrams is to ensure that your reader stays engaged with what the outcome will be, as you can see with these two examples.

Chapter 2: Building Your Plot

Now that you are aware of how a plot should look, it is time to begin building your own! In this chapter, we are going to explore the various steps of building your own plot line. You will be given all of the information you need to move from start to finish effectively. Even if you are not already aware of what your story is going to be, you will be given the opportunity to generate an idea within' this chapter. This chapter is all about helping you come up with a great idea and transform it into a powerful plot line that will help you generate a moving and engaging story that keeps your readers invested until the very end.

Step One: Get Inspired

The first part of writing a plot for your story is to get inspired. If you haven't already got an idea of what you want your story to be about, look for inspiration to help you pick a topic. You can find inspiration for stories in all areas of life from your day-to-day life to stories that other people tell you. You may even be able to reflect back on certain parts of your life or the life of someone you know and draw on experiences to help you become inspired on what you should write your book about. Alternatively, you may draw inspiration from other stories that you have heard or read. Ensure that when you are picking your story, however, that you don't directly copy someone else's story as this is a form of plagiarism. If you are drawing on inspiration from a story you've already heard or read before, take the time to look at the story from unique angles to see how you could write the same story only from a completely different perspective, potentially even with a different outcome altogether.

If you already have an idea of what you want to write your story about, take the time now to elaborate on that idea in your head. Look at it from all angles and see how you can ensure that you have a rich topic that will provide you with the opportunity to draw on it for plenty of material and substance to build your story from. You want to make sure that you have the entire idea of the story beforehand so that you have a general idea of where to go during the writing process. While you can certainly go ahead without a general idea, you will be losing all purposes of writing a plot line. And, ultimately, you will end up writing a story with no sense of direction that may result in you having a very bland, unexciting and otherwise boring story.

Step Two: Getting Direction

Now that you have generated your idea for what you want to write about, it is time to give yourself a sense of direction. This will ensure that you are clear on the focus of your story so that you can remain focused during the writing process. Creating a sense of direction for your story is extremely simple. Once you have generated the entire idea of what you want your story to be about, simply sum it all up into one sentence. Being able to sum it up in a single sentence means that you have clarity on what your story is and you are also clear on what the outcome will be. The outcome is ultimately what you need to know to have a sense of direction as this is what you are going to be writing toward. Below are a few examples of sentences that identify the entire plot of a story in a few words.

"An estranged sister returns to her brother's life so she can take his money and buy her way out of a dangerous situation."

"A bartender falls deeper in love with a regular patron each time he visits her bar and eventually they fall in love, get married, and buy the bar."

"A surgeon who is murdered by his patient that is a victim of neurotic episodes was believed to be a tragic victim, but later they discover that he was actually holding some very sensitive information that ultimately got him killed."

As you can see, each of these sentences gives a very direct insight as to what the story is going to be about and who is involved. It shows you who the protagonists are and what the outcome is for each of them. By identifying what the outcome is and whom it belongs to help give you, the writer, a sense of direction in regards to where you are going with your story. This sense of direction is what you want to keep in mind during the entire writing process as all events, thoughts, conversations, and other actions should ultimately lead up to it.

Step Three: Turning Your Idea into a Story

Once you have an idea and a sense of direction, it is time to turn your idea into a story. A great way to work with this part of the process is to start with the very basics and then build from there. That being said, start by writing down what you already know about your story. Anything you have already planned, brainstorm it on a piece of paper. Next, turn this brainstorm into some basic plot points. Be sure to add some twists, turns, unexpected events, wins, and losses along the way. Then, when you have completed that, take another piece of paper and write these points out along a plot line. If you are using lined paper, leave a few lines between each point. Don't worry about how you are going to organize these onto the story arc, they don't need to be in chronological form just yet. Instead, focus on getting them written down. Once you have, then you can start elaborating on the details of each of these points. Consider how each plot point contributes to the greater story and what should be involved so that it can contribute in a strong way. The best way to look at it is to view these unique plot points as tools. Each one will be used to drive your story forward and tell a certain part of it. You want to ensure that these tools are equipped with all of the pieces that they will need to provide a strong driving factor for your story. You don't necessarily need to know all of the factors of the story, but you should be taking the time to learn as much as possible. Ideally, you want to have at least 4-6 sentences about each plot point where you identify as many details about that plot point as you can. Remember, they don't need to be in chronological order so simply make sure that you are writing down anything that comes to mind that would be important to the story itself. As you are writing, you may find that you are in need of additional plot points so be sure that you take the time to brainstorm these and elaborate on them as well. This will ensure that you have all of the substance you need to generate a strong plot for your story.

Step Four: Create Your Story Arc

Now, you want to begin creating your story arc. This is going to be the outline that was described in chapter one, with the exposition, rising action, climax, falling action, and resolution. You can write this in list form by identifying each element of the arc, or you can draw it out on a piece of paper so that you can plan out your plot as though you are creating a timeline for your novel. Each method works, and in fact, it may be beneficial for you to do both, starting with the list and then moving over to the diagram, if you feel that you do better with the opportunity to both plan it out on a list and then get an idea of the final effect on the diagram.

Creating your story arc this way is what will ultimately give you the opportunity to get an idea of how your story looks overall. For this part, you want to step back from your detailing and look at the greater picture. Here is where you are going to identify where each plot point fits on the diagram, and where it should be placed in relevance to the other events taking place. Before you get started with placing anything on your diagram, read steps six and seven as they will provide you with important information about how you can do this effectively.

Step Six: Start with The End

When it comes to creating your plot, you want to start with the end. Remember, this is the direction you are heading in, and this is where you want your story to end up. You should be able to get an idea of what your end is going to look like based on the focus sentence you generated in step two. Now, however, you want to elaborate on that. This is going to be the first official plot point you outline on your story arc. Fortunately, it is an easy one. This point lies at the end of the map, so you can place it at the very end of your story arc. Once you have, identify what needs to happen in order for you to know that the end has been reached. What that means is identify the conditions, the state of mind, and any other relevant information that will take place at the end of the book that will be an indicating factor to you that the story has matured and is now ready to be ended.

As you read in step five, it is not necessary for you to go into specific detail about this point altogether as this should have already happened in step three when you were describing and elaborating on each plot point. Instead, simply refer back to that brainstorm if you need more information about all of the details surrounding the ending of your story.

Step Seven: Organize Your Plot Points on the Story Arc

Once you have identified the end-point, you want to start organizing the remaining plot points along your story arc. Now, this is the part where you need to pay attention. Here is where you may choose to put less detail into it if you want, especially if there are certain elements that you simply don't know yet, but ultimately having this plan created in the way that we are about to explore is what will ensure that you are clear on the focus and direction of your book and what you need to do to arrive at the outcome.

You want to start by working backward along the plot points. Pay attention to what your end point is, and then write everything on the line going backward from there. Reverse engineering your plotline in this way will ensure that you cover all of the important plot factors and that everything happens chronologically *for* your outcome, rather than it randomly appearing out of nowhere. Doing this actively ensures that everything makes sense and that it is built in the most solid form possible. It also ensures that your plot contains all of the information that is needed, and that you can easily find where each plot point belongs based on what needs to happen *before* the last plot point in order for it to have even occurred in the first place. For example, in order for the bank robber to rob the bank, he must first plan the robbery, therefore placing the plan *before* the action. Use this frame of thinking for each of your plot points, and they will all fall together on the line effortlessly.

Step Eight: Tying it All Together

Once you have successfully identified all of the different plot points, step back and take a look at your overall story arc. Pay attention to the different points you have included, and where everything falls. If it is too crowded, you may consider eliminating some of the less important plot points from the story arc so that you are not going further than what actually is required for the story itself. Alternatively, if you notice anything is missing take this time to identify what it is and include it in your story arc. Once you have, review it one more time to make sure all of the elements fit on it well and that they are all contributing to the overall story itself.

Finally, the best way to bring it all together is to write a few sentences about your story arc. Essentially you want to give an overview of your story based strictly on each plot point you have added on the story arc. For example, "Angela is a barista who has been working for a local coffee shop for six years. She recently met a new friend, Sam, who has been getting her into a lot of trouble. Her boss was worried about her, but this only made Angela feel guilty. To avoid the guilt, she quit her job as a barista and pursued a job in a sketchy nightclub with Sam. This lead to the girls being taken advantage of by a patron of the club, which ultimately leads them to find themselves in a basement of an unknown building." You would carry on writing sentences that walk you through each plotline along the way as this helps you see the flow of how your story will go. Obviously, you want to go into much more detail when writing the story and actually bring the reader along with you. However, writing it in this way allows you to see everything and make sure it all works together well. It can also help you identify anywhere that your plot may need to be altered, reorganized, strengthened, or otherwise adjusted to benefit the overall story.

It is vital that you take the time to look over the entire plotline after it has been laid out because this is what will ensure that you have made the best one possible. Of course, your plotline doesn't need to be intensely elaborate and overdone, but having it clearly defined and knowing the important details of each plot point will ensure that you have plenty to write about. It also helps ensure that you are clear on the direction of your story and that you don't end up going off track somewhere during the writing process. Furthermore, if you find that you are feeling stuck from an episode of writer's block, you can consult your plot line to help you move forward and stay on track with your writing.

Creating your plotline can take anywhere from a few hours to a few days. It all depends on how much time you are willing to invest in the process and how much you already know, or don't know, about your story. For some people, getting the inspiration for the story itself can take a few days or even weeks. Don't be discouraged if you find that this isn't a quick one-afternoon job for you. The best stories take time to accumulate, and they are well-planned in advance. The more prepared you are now, the stronger your story will be in the long run. While you don't need to plan so deeply that you take away any opportunity for you to be creative during the writing process, it certainly benefits to have clarity around your book, your goals, and what you envision the end result to be with your story.

Chapter 3: Bringing Your Plot to Life

Bringing your plot to life happens entirely through the writing process. However, there are many ways that you can ensure that you activate the right techniques during this process to really bring your plot to life. Ultimately, bringing your plot to life is the process of taking your story from being an outline on a page to being an actual book that moves your readers and keeps them engaged and invested in your book all the way until the end. In this chapter, we are going to identify important tips to consider when it comes to writing around your plot to ensure that it comes to life effectively for your reader.

Consider How Your Characters Fit In

Your characters are the voice to your story. They are also the tools you use to move your story from point to point. This makes them an extremely important element of your story overall. You will learn more about in-depth character development in the book "Character Development" of this series, but in the meantime, you should consider how they fit in overall. This is the part where you want to consider how each character is going to fit into the plot points, as well as how they will be affected by them. Primarily, you want to think about how each point will affect your protagonist and your antagonist. The more you are aware of how they are being affected, the easier it will be for you to write a compelling story that has your readers genuinely believing each point.

Since you haven't already established the in-depth portion of your characters, you should consider them in a general sense. For example, "In chapter six, Elise moves away which causes Jonathan to feel lost. Elise is affected by this move because she is moving away from her best friend and into a place where she doesn't know anyone. Jonathan is affected because he has a crush on Elise but he never managed to say anything before she left and now he doesn't think he will ever get the opportunity to tell her how she truly feels. He knows pursuing her dream career is good for her, but he can't help but feel a sense of guilt and hopelessness around the entire situation."

It is important that you consider your characters in each situation because this will help you get inside of their head more. This is important for character development, which you will learn about, but it is also important for story development. You want to make sure that the events move forward in a way that flows and is natural for the characters within' your story. If you are unsure about how to consider your characters in various plot points, use this generic question: "How does x affect y because of z?" For example, "How does moving affect Jonathan because of his love for Elise?" This question will help get you thinking about how each part of the book affects your characters and then plan out how you can use this in both the planning and writing processes.

Hide the Plot Effectively

When you are writing a plot, it is important that you learn to hide the plot effectively. Even though most readers are aware that there is a climax that typically involves some form of large conflict in virtually every book, it doesn't mean that they want to see the points of the plot sloppily put into every part of the book. Instead, they want to read the book and have that as a natural flow that is hidden in the background. Seamlessly hiding the plot within' your book requires a fair amount of practice, as well as a few techniques. One you will learn in the next section, which involves effectively transitioning between plot points. Another includes giving enough detail to each plot point within' the book that it is well discussed and does not feel as though it has been rushed through. Rushing through plot points detracts from the quality of your book and takes away from the reader experience by not giving them enough information about each plot point. You want to make sure that your reader understands why each element of the story exists and how it ultimately contributes to the story itself. It should feel as though the flow is moving naturally, not slow and not rushed.

Hiding the plot sequencing and story arc within' your story effectively means that your reader should not be able to easily identify when the next major story plot is coming, or what it will be. If you are not using a dynamic plot line and hiding it effectively, there is a good chance that your reader will be able to identify what your story is and determine the major plot points and outcome well before they ever got to those parts of the story. This takes away from the reading experience and generally leads to them putting the book down and not finishing it because they simply can't stay engaged. Effectively building and hiding your plotline avoids this.

Effective Transitioning Between Plot Points

It is important that you learn to effectively transition between plot points. If you are not highly practiced with this, you may want to identify what will take place during the transitions *before* you begin writing. These transition phases are heavily important to the story overall because they contribute to the natural flow of the story. Think about it, your life is not a series of major events. There are several things that take place in between the major things that happen in your life. The day-to-day events. While you don't want to bore your readers by repetitively sharing the same day over and over throughout the story, you also want to make sure that you give insight to your character's daily lives and what the calm is like between the storm. Take the time to naturally transition the plot along the major points, rather than simply jumping from one to the next. This is what gives your story a natural flow and prevents it from sounding stiff or uncomfortable.

There are many ways that you can transition between different plot elements, several of which will arise naturally as you are writing. However, the following points will give you some ideas as to how you can transition points if you are feeling stuck.

- Talk about day-to-day life, but switch it up with each transition that you use this strategy for. You may refer back to certain points, but don't explain the exact same events in great detail over and over. Instead, highlight different elements of the day-to-day experiences in between each transition.

- End the chapter and start the next one. While you don't want to use this strategy every time, it is a great way to start suspense. Make sure you don't jump right into the climax of the next plot point with the new chapter, but rather that you build up to it from a new angle than you would have with where you were previously. This also helps build suspense.

- Talk about the falling action from the previous plot point and then transition into the rising action of the next plot point.

You want to change up which strategy you use each time you are conducting a transition as using the same ones frequently can result in the book becoming predictable. While new chapters should bring new plot points, for example, they shouldn't happen at exactly the same time with the new chapter. You should not immediately feast into the rising action and place the climax of the new plot point within' the first page or two of the chapter. Instead, let the rising action linger, or even blend together two unique transition strategies for greater impact. The more you vary your approach and use unique angles, the better your overall story will be.

Have Action-Packed Plot Points

Plot points are meant to move the story forward, and while not all of them will be action-packed, you should certainly have a fair bit that it. Action-packed plot points encourage the reader to become further engaged in your book. They become interested in what is happening, how it ties into what has already happened, and what it could mean for the characters going forward. Effectively action-packed plot points littered throughout your story keeps it active and engaging for your readers, and it also helps move you forward toward the outcome. Action is where the motion is, so you want to use this tool as a strategy to help you move the story forward.

When you are using action-packed plot points, make sure you don't go too overboard. First, you want to have some of your plot points that are built differently, such as around emotional points. This will ensure that your reader doesn't become overwhelmed with action. Second, you want to make sure that the action makes sense to the story, that it moves the story forward, and that it doesn't overwhelm the reader. Using too much action can result in your reader feeling overwhelmed and struggling to keep up with your story. It also leads to them feeling disconnected from the story because they simply cannot relate to it; it doesn't seem like a realistic situation that would ever happen and therefore they are pulled out of the story.

Using action-packed plot points is a great tool that does not need to be used sparingly, but it does need to be used effectively. If you are interested in how you can add these to your story, consider looking at your overall plot and seeing where the action-based plot points are. Pay attention to what the action is, how it affects the story, and how you might be able to infuse more action into each plot point to get the most of it. However, make sure you keep a few that feature action but still have a more profound sense to them. These are the ones where something major happens, but it's not necessarily built around "and then, and then, and then." Instead, there is a large event that takes place which isn't clouded by several other events. This is a great way to make an event more profound, so if you need a certain plot point to carry a lot of meaning, make this one of the ones where there is less action built into it and more emotion built into it instead.

Make the Plot Engage the Reader's Emotions

In addition to having a plot that uses action to drive the story forward, have a plot that activates various emotions within' the reader to keep them engaged. Emotional attachment is what encourages a reader to stay connected to the story. When they develop a sense of attachment and concern for the protagonist, as well as some form of emotional resentment against the antagonist, readers are more likely to stay engaged in the book. Because they are genuinely invested in knowing how things turn out for the characters within' the book, they are more compelled to keep reading.

You can engage the reader's emotions in a variety of ways, but ultimately how you do so will be a part of your plot building. This is also a large part of what brings the plot to life for people. If they do not have a reason to care, they simply won't care. Instead, they will tune out. When you give people a reason to care, however, they are more interested, and therefore the entire story comes to life and fuels a passion within' them to carry forward. They feel empathy for your characters, and therefore you have the power to engage other emotions within' them to further draw them in and keep them moving forward.

The best way to engage emotions is to use the characters at each plot point to do so. For example, if someone dies in one of the plot points you can use the reactions of the characters to spark emotions such as relief, grief, anger, or otherwise. How you choose to spark emotions heavily relies on your decision, as well as where you want the story to go. This is all about the outcome, remember. You should seek to activate several of your reader's emotions throughout the duration of the story. While you don't want to infuse too many emotions into each situation, the story as a whole should dance on the emotional heartstrings of your readers in many different ways. The more emotional the experience is, the more enjoyable the read is.

Once again, you want to make sure that you are using emotions within' reason. You shouldn't be attempting to forcefully push your readers into extreme states of any given emotion. Instead, you want to suggest emotions through the actions, reactions, words, and thoughts of your characters and allow your reader to take it the extra mile on their own. Pushing it too hard can make it feel forced and unnatural, therefore taking away from the reading experience itself. You want the emotion to be believable, natural, and aligned with the story you are telling in each given moment throughout the book. When it comes to generating emotional reactions from your readers, you want to look at the book as a whole. See how you can use emotions overall, rather than how you can use them in each given moment. This will help you move your reader through emotions in a natural, well-developed way.

When it comes to infusing emotions, there is typically a certain way that emotions are infused into a plot line. In the beginning, readers are given opportunities to develop emotional attachments to the characters, so you want to emphasize on empathy in this part of the book. When you build empathy effectively here, you give your readers a reason to care for the rest of the book.

Next, you want to play on that empathy to generate a healthy connection between the characters and your reader as you are building the rising action in your plot line. Here, you want to use a lot of positive and happy emotions. You also want to use some feelings of sadness, grief, anxiety, anger, fear, and other emotions to help build up a sense of what the stakes mean for your character. These emotions also help build suspense and get your reader emotionally invested in the conflicts that are happening to your characters.

At the climax, you want to have a lot of energy built up. The specific emotion you emphasize on will depend on your unique genre. It may be love, anger, relief, resentment, frustration, fear, anxiety, or any other number of emotions depending on your genre and the story you are telling. This emotion is the one you want to charge the most as it is the highest point of your story. Therefore your reader really needs to *feel* like it is while they are reading.

As you move through the falling action, you want to highlight emotions like empathy, grief, sorrow, relief, and other emotions that you would typically feel after something major has finally happened. Again, the exact emotions you will use will be unique to your unique story. There are also a few important emotions you want to infuse into this part of your story. This part of your story should particularly focus on hope, faith, forgiveness, and rebuilding and moving forward with their lives. Since this is the path towards the resolution, you want them to genuinely feel that the resolution is coming and that the character feels hopeful for it, too. While they may lose hope sometimes, it should be a lingering emotion in the background.

When the novel ends, you typically want to give the reader a sense of closure. This is where you can give them the "happily ever after" that most readers come for. This could be a happily ever after where the characters truly achieved happier lives, or it could be one where they live the happiest version of their life that they possibly can based on the traumatic experiences that the characters recently endured. Once again, this will heavily depend on your story and the genre you are writing in. For example, romantic novels typically end in a feel-good happily ever after where the two lovers end up together and lead charmingly romantic lives until their old age. Alternatively, a mystery novel where someone is murdered in the beginning and the duration of the novel is spent discovering who did it should have a happily ever after whereby the murderer is found, the case is solved, justice is served, and the characters can move on with their healing process.

Chapter 4: Best Plot Building Advice

The basic plot-building advice and the eight-step process in chapter 2 give you a great foundation for creating your plot outline. However, you want to make sure that you take it that extra step further and have a great plot outline, and not just a "done" one. The following advice will help give you an insight as to how you can strengthen your plot and create a powerful one that will drive your story forward. These tips and tricks are provided from some of the best writers themselves, so you can trust that they are sound and will help you with building and troubleshooting your own plot!

Never Skip the Plot Building Process

The first tip you should know is that you never want to skip the plot building process. Even if you already know most of the information you want to share in your mind, you still want to build the plot. Building a plot allows you to get the information out of your mind and take it from a great plot to a phenomenal one. This process enables you to go deeper, question yourself and your intentions, and increase the quality of the plot overall. It also ensures that you can organize it and stay focused so that your story remains on track. It truly is essential in generating a well-structured, chronological and focused plot line that will drive your story forward and keep readers engaged.

Failing to create a plot line is truly a tragedy when it comes to your results. It often leads to the story lacking the depth that it could have, and ultimately not reaching its full potential. Because you didn't allow yourself to further explore your purpose, your plan, and your direction, you were never able to elaborate on it and strengthen it in a way that would serve your story even more than your initial idea already did. It can also lead to your story being sloppy, disorganized, and all over the place in such a way that your readers simply cannot follow, and therefore they fail to become engaged and stay invested in reading your book. If you want to have a book that makes sense, that engages your readers, and that has them craving more of your work, then you absolutely must start with a plot outline.

Build Strong Characters to Compliment Your Plot

Your plot is only as strong as your characters are. If you build a strong plot but fail to generate the right characters that can be used to drive the plot forward, you are not going to have a great story. Having a strong story that your readers will love ultimately comes from focusing on all elements of the story, including the plot. You should not primarily focus on the plot, the characters, the structure, or any other element of the story. Instead, you want to make sure that each individual part is well-developed so that they all work together like a well-oiled machine. Not only does this make the writing process easier, but it also maximizes the quality of your book and ensures that it reaches its fullest potential in all aspects.

Your characters are the ones that are involved in the plot, and they are the ones that you are speaking and acting through to drive it forward. If they are not developed enough, are not created specifically for the plot, or otherwise struggle to carry your plot forward, you are not going to have an incredible story. In fact, you may not even have a great one. Instead, you may have a mediocre one that was lost on characters who were not strong enough to carry the story forward. In the next book, you will learn about how you can develop your own characters, and you will also be walked through an in-depth character building exercise that allows you to generate the best possible characters. Ensure that you take the time to use that and build characters specifically for your story and plotline so that they carry it forward and lead you towards complete success with your book.

Have a Powerful Outcome

The outcome of your story is what it's all about. Literally, the entire story building up to that point is only there for that specific point. People want to know how things turn out for all of the characters involved so they remain invested until the end, curious about what the outcome will be. If your outcome is not powerful enough, your readers are going to be heavily disappointed. There are a few things to keep in mind when it comes to developing your outcome, which we will explore now.

First, you want to avoid your outcome being too "flat" for the story. It should be full of some form of emotion that leaves your reader genuinely feeling something when the book ends.

They should feel hopeful, grateful, happy, or otherwise positive about the ending of the story. Additionally, they should feel as though they have been granted with closure from the ending. Your reader should feel that all loose ends have been tied and that anything that was lingering in the story was explained before you drew the story to a close. They should be feeling satisfied and complete with the story you have provided, and not like they are left wondering about any other element. Unless, of course, you are purposefully ending on a cliffhanger to help draw them into the next book of a series, you want to avoid leaving your readers with a cliffhanger. Instead, you want to provide them with a sound ending that makes them feel happy for the character like their goal was achieved because they accomplished what they had set out to accomplish in the beginning when we were presented with the primary problem.

When you are generating your outcome, you also want to make sure that it leaves a powerful impact on your reader. This comes from the emotions, but it should come from the thoughts as well. A great way to do this is to leave them reflecting on a part of their own life, reflecting on the story itself, or even feeling as though they have learned a lesson through the reading process. The ending should be sort of like a grand finale for your reader, complete with a drum roll and fireworks.

Use a Natural Ending Point

To elaborate on how to end your story, you want to ensure that you choose a natural ending point. You do not want to pick a spot that feels unnatural like something has been left unsaid, or like the reader isn't getting the full gist of the story. You also don't want to carry on well after the natural ending point has come as this will dilute the quality of your ending. Instead, you want to make sure that you keep it powerful by providing plenty of information, but only the necessary information. It is important that you remember that the outcome is the part of the book that will remain freshest in your readers mind so this is the part that should have the biggest impact on them.

Let Your Characters Resolve Their Own Conflict

Many stories fall flat when they let a force of nature or some unknown hero come in and save their characters from the problems that have arisen throughout the story. In some cases, this helps. In the majority, however, it is a very weak technique that takes away from the story. Readers are drawn into a story because they develop a connection to the character. So, naturally, they want to watch the character develop and see the natural conflict resolution by the character. They want to know how this has changed them, how it has helped them grow, and what they have learned from it. Not only does this allow the reader to feel as though they are spying through a peephole into the life of the character, but when done properly it also helps the reader learn some things from the character, too. When readers feel connected to the character, it is often because they relate in some way. Therefore, when the character naturally evolves, it causes the reader to look within' themselves and see how they have grown, or how they might grow in the future as a result of what they have witnessed in your characters. For this to happen, however, there has to be a change in your character that takes place naturally. This means that it is important that you let your character resolve their own conflict. While you can allow heroes and random acts of nature take the credit on smaller subplots within' the story, it is important that the major changes and lessons are directly through the character themselves.

Be Original

If the story you are writing has already been written and you are only changing the names and a few basic points in the book, you are going to lose traction with readers. Books that are outstanding and that become known as great and even phenomenal books are ones that are written out of originality. Everything else gets tossed in the bargain bin within' a few days from their launch. You want to make sure that you are writing an original story that your reader will not feel like they have already read. If they feel like the story is too similar to another one they have read, then your story becomes both predictable and unexciting. You may even damage your writing reputation by essentially copying someone else's work. And, if you're not careful, you could infringe on plagiarism rules. It is important that you generate an original plot that your reader doesn't know from previous stories. While it will certainly share similarities to others in the genre and it may borrow some ideas or techniques from other books, the overall product should be unique and original from what has already been written and released. This will ensure that you keep your readers engaged and interested throughout the reading process and that your story has the potential to climb to best-seller rating, rather than simply be skimmed through and dropped just as quickly.

Use an Exciting Plot

Readers don't *want* to get engaged with your book, they *need* to. If you use a plot that lacks excitement, you are going to struggle to get your readers engaged, and therefore you will fail to meet their expectations and have them raving about your book. Instead, they will simply close the book and won't recommend it to anyone else. Or, worse, they will leave a negative review on reviewing platforms about your book, discouraging others from giving it a chance, too. What you need is an exciting plot that will keep your readers engaged and invested from the time they open the book until the time they finish reading it. Your readers should feel like they don't want to put the book down when they're reading it, and like they can't wait to get back to it once they have. They should be heavily invested in the characters, the stakes, the conflicts, and the story itself. Doing this requires you to have an exciting plot.

An exciting plot is one that moves forward. It should not go straight from point A to point B, though. Instead, it should take many unexpected twists, turns, and side steps as it advances towards the final outcome. The reader should not know what to expect, but they should be emotionally invested in each part of it. Every plot point that you include should contribute to the overall story in some way, even if the reader doesn't understand how right away, or until much later. The more effectively you keep the story exciting and interesting, the more you will generate raving readers who are eager to share your book with others and encourage them to give it a read themselves.

Switch Up the Pace

When it comes to writing a fiction novel, you always want to emphasize on how it compares to reality. Even if you are writing a fantasy novel, the pace at which the book moves should be comparable to reality itself. There should be parts where it is fast, and parts where it moves slower. There should be areas where strong emotions are sparked, and there should be areas where no emotions are sparked. Your reader should feel as though the book ebbs and flows, much like an ocean tide. This gives them the opportunity to move along with the story at a natural, realistic pace. During the times of action and emotion they are heavily engaged and are rapidly being fed new information, and during the times of calm and more relaxing emotions, they are given the opportunity to reflect on recent events while also seeing how the characters are doing the same. Switching up the pace gives your book a realistic flow that keeps readers believing it to be true and maintains their ability to relate to it in some way at most times.

Stay On Track

Subplots are a great way to add depth to your book. However, too many can result in your book going off track and becoming confusing to the reader. You should not be darting around with information, sharing too many subplots, or diving into information that is entirely irrelevant to the overall story. Instead, you want to make sure that you are staying focused on the end result. Any subplot that somehow contributes to the overall story by giving it depth, allowing you to further explain certain elements of people or the plot, or otherwise increasing the quality of your story should be considered. Those that add enough value that makes them worthwhile should be kept. All other subplots should be ignored. When it comes to staying focused, make sure that you never divulge into information that is entirely irrelevant to the story. Unless it is drawing the reader towards the outcome, teaching them more about your characters, or otherwise providing them with a value that contributes to the story itself, you should not be sharing it. Getting carried away with irrelevant information results in your reader becoming confused. It dilutes your story and makes your readers want to close the book because they simply don't grasp what you're trying to tell them.

Have A Strong "Why"

Your "why" is your outcome. It is the reason why you are writing the story. Are you writing it to teach people who murdered the person in the beginning? Are you writing it to share a romantic love story between two people? Are you doing it to dive deeper into a fantasy world that you have built in your imagination and to bring life to it? Are you doing it to teach your reader a lesson? Why are you writing your book? Knowing why the book is being written in the first place can help with a significant number of writing elements. Your why is ultimately what will help you generate your plot as it will ensure that you are creating plot points that are relevant to the overall story, or the "why." It also ensures that your story stays focused. Furthermore, it helps your readers feel the significance of your novel. Your "why" for writing it will also be their "why" for reading it. They need to feel the significance and impact of this so that they feel compelled to read your book in the first place and to continue reading it until it ends. This is how they will get the biggest impact from your book, so you want to make sure that you are clear as to why you are writing it in the first place.

Don't Abuse Writing Techniques

Writing techniques are like tools that you use to structure your story, create certain causes and effects, and ultimately design your entire story in a way that impacts the reader the way the story is intended to. They are an incredible selection of tools that you absolutely need to use to generate a phenomenal story that your readers will love. However, you have to be aware when using these techniques. You never want to abuse them by overusing them, using them in the wrong area, or otherwise misusing them. When they are not used properly, these techniques take away from the story, and you dilute their impact overall. It is important that you use the right techniques in the right places and that you don't overuse them so as to eliminate the effect they have on your story.

Learn as You Go

One of the best pieces of advice that can be given is to learn as you go. Don't be afraid to make mistakes, take on criticism, and increase your skill by actively practicing it. Remember, you can't learn something if you don't practice in the first place. You don't try something and become an overnight master with it. You have to use the skill, practice the skill, and expand on the skill as regularly as possible if you are going to become a master at it. The best writers got to where they are today by practicing, listening to feedback, and improving their own skills. One great way to go about it is to keep a notebook and write down feedback you get, as well as ideas or thoughts you have along the way. This gives you something solid to look back on and reflect on when it comes to increasing your skill and doing better in the future.

Conclusion

Thank you for reading *"Plot Writing: Step-by-Step | Essential Story Plotting, Conflict Writing and Plotline Tricks Any Writer Can Learn"*. This book was designed to help you take your plot deeper, increase your writing skills, and give your story a greater sense of purpose to keep your reader engaged and entertained along the way.

I hope this book was able to provide you with new, revolutionary, and insightful tips and tricks to help you with your plot. I also hope that you were able to use the eight-step plot building guide to help you generate a plot that will powerfully drive your story so that you can create the next best-seller. Remember, these tips are ones that can take you to the next level, but it is up to you to implement and practice them if you are going to take it all the way. Only you have the power to materialize the stories in your head and share them with the world! Practicing will help you do this with maximum impact.

The next step is to create your own plot line that will enrich your story and carry it to the end. Remember, reverse engineering is the best way to ensure that your story features everything it requires, so always look at things backward, if not starting backwards to begin with. Additionally, make sure that you take the time to read the next book where you will learn to develop incredible characters that will compliment your plot perfectly and help you take your book to the top. Recall that a book is like a well-oiled machine whereby all of the elements such as the structure, plot line, outline, and characters are built together to operate seamlessly and create a relatable, realistic story that your readers will love. Each element should be individually developed with the intention of it being a part of the greater story so that they contribute to the greatness of your novel.

Thank you, and good luck!

STORY STRUCTURE

STEP-BY-STEP

ESSENTIAL STORY BUILDING, STORY DEVELOPMENT AND SUSPENSE WRITING TRICKS ANY WRITER CAN LEARN

SANDY MARSH

BOOK 2: STORY STRUCTURE

STEP-BY-STEP

Essential Story Building, Story Development and Suspense Writing Tricks Any Writer Can Learn

Sandy Marsh

reparation, damages, or monetary loss due to the information herein, either directly or indirectly.

Respective authors own all copyrights not held by the publisher.

The information herein is offered for informational purposes solely, and is universal as so. The presentation of the information is without contract or any type of guarantee assurance.

The trademarks that are used are without any consent, and the publication of the trademark is without permission or backing by the trademark owner. All trademarks and brands within this book are for clarifying purposes only and are the owned by the owners themselves, not affiliated with this document.

Table of Contents

Introduction

Thank you and congratulations on purchasing *"Story Structure: Step-by-Step | Essential Story Building, Story Development and Suspense Writing Tricks Any Writer Can Learn"*.

This book was created to help you learn a series of tips and tricks that will help you enrich your story and make it a must-read book for your target audience. By using these techniques and strategies in your own book you will be able to generate a storyline that is rich with suspense, action, and other tools that are important to keep your readers engaged and excited about reading your book.

Each chapter within' this book is dedicated to one element of story structures themselves, ensuring that you are provided with the greatest in-depth detail to ensure that you learn plenty to help you produce a phenomenal story. Before the book ends, you will be provided with tips from top writers and authors that will help you write like the pros.

This book was not designed for any particular experience level when it comes to writing. Instead, it has been populated with tricks that will help any writer from beginner to advanced. If you are someone who typically struggles to write stories but you are looking to get yours heard, you can be certain that you will learn some tips here to help you get on your way towards having your book completed. Likewise, if you have done this before but are looking for a refresher or are otherwise interested in learning more to enrich your story and create an addictive read for your audience, you are certainly going to learn something also.

Please be sure to take your time and work through all of the tips and tricks provided within' this book. While some may not be entirely relevant to the work you are producing, they may provide you with inspiration to move forward in a more powerful way. As well, be sure to keep this book handy for future writing ventures as you never know which part will stand out each time. Finally, remember that writing is an experience that should be enjoyed by both the reader and the author. Be sure that you take the time to make the process enjoyable for yourself so that you can produce your best work. And finally, have fun!

Chapter 1: Purpose of Story Structure

Understanding the purpose of story structure will ensure that you are aware of how it can make (or break) your story, and why it is so crucial that you develop a strong structure within' your own story. Prior to diving into any important tips or strategies, we are going to explore what a story structure is, exactly, and what purpose it serves within' your story.

What is a Story Structure?

In basic form, a story structure is essentially a map that is drawn to take your reader from point a to point b. You want them to start at the beginning of the book and end at the end, only after being taken through an experience which is essentially each "stop" on the map. This map is used to help identify how people solve different problems, as well as to assist in conveying the message that the author is attempting to send from the storytelling process. In essence, the structure of your story is the process where the outline is transformed from being a simple idea to being the bones of your story. It becomes the part that holds the entire story up and gives it a form that is both natural, yet moving.

Where do Story Structures Come from?

Story structure is less of an invention or creation and more of an element of the story that was observed and thus plucked from the process and used as a tool to help generate new stories. For thousands of years, humans have been telling stories to one another whilst using story structure without ever knowing what it actually was. This is the part of the story that was used to draw listeners or readers forward through the story while keeping them actively engaged and wanting to know more. With the use of story structure, storytellers were able to walk people through the process of the story, rather than simply telling them the beginning and end factors. This meant that storytelling became an experience, both for the teller and the listener or reader. It was all thanks to story structure.

Although people weren't aware of what story structure actually was in the beginning, the idea of it emerged over time. It was identified as the structure of the story that was used to describe how certain characters within' the story dealt with problems and overcame them, as well as how they interacted with and communicated with other individuals from the story.

After identifying the concept of story structure and observing it from ancient storytelling experiences, people began using it as a general guideline for the process of building stories. Now, your story structure involves important information about the setting of your story, the people involved, the conflicts they experience, and how they overcome said conflicts. It is essentially every part of your story pulled together and planned out in a specific structure that helps you as the author understand what story you are trying to tell before and during the writing process.

Why You Need One

Having a story structure may seem pointless, especially if you already have the story in your head and you are simply attempting to get it out on paper. However, story structures are extremely valuable and can help you with the entire storytelling process. They are excellent for helping you identify how you are going to deliver the story to ensure that the reader receives the story effectively. This is more than simply providing the reader with information to help walk them from point a to point b. Instead, it is about giving them this relevant information in such a way that they are eager to know more and they stay actively engaged with the storytelling process.

When you design your story structure it helps you identify what your story sounds like to other people when they are reading it. It is important that you develop one before you start writing so that you have a strong execution plan going into the writing process. While you can simply write the story from your mind, this may result in you not emphasizing strong points enough, or otherwise diluting your story with information that takes away from it having a strong structure. Instead, you could plan your story out on paper first and essentially lay out the points that you will take your readers through within' the story. This way you can walk yourself through it and learn more about your story in advance. Doing this gives you the opportunity to identify any weak points and strengthen them, to ensure that your story makes sense and flows well, and to develop confidence in the idea that you have generated a strong enough plotline that your readers are going to stay actively engaged and enjoy the reading experience.

Now that you are more clear on what a story structure is and why it is so crucial to the writing process, it is time to explore the process of actually creating your own story structure so that you can embark on writing your own story. The following chapters will walk you through the step-by-step process of building your own story structure, as well as every technique you should know in order to have a strong structure that will leave your readers wanting more.

Chapter 2: The Essentials of Building a Structure

The first part of generating your own story structure is understanding the essentials. In this chapter, we are going to explore all of the basics that you should know when it comes to creating your own story structure. Throughout this chapter, you will be provided with tips and techniques to help you design the foundation of your structure. By the end, you should have a solid structure that will help you produce a phenomenal story.

9 Step Process

Most stories follow a typical nine-step process in order to generate their story structure. Some people prefer to alternate how the structure is designed, such as by introducing the climax in the first portion of the book. Still, they typically tend to break the book up into three main parts, or "acts" as they are called. This helps keep each part of the book focused on a certain subject that ultimately contributes to the overall story.

The following sections will introduce each step of the nine-step process and how they should be executed in order to produce a high-quality story structure. Please note that these are following the traditional method based on how many other stories have been structured throughout the ages. You may choose to alternate yours if you are more advanced, but if you are new to storytelling you will likely want to stick to and master this traditional structure before venturing into other structures. This will provide you with more practice towards developing a structure and using the purpose of the structure to your advantage. Once you are more skilled with structures then you can start to create alternative ones for your future stories because you will have a stronger idea about what makes them work and what doesn't.

Step One: First Act

The first step is to introduce the first act. This is the part of the story where you want to introduce the reader to your characters, the setting you have chosen, and anything that is at stake in the story. This is where they understand what is important and why. In the first act, you are given the opportunity to catch the attention of the reader and give them a reason to care about what story you are telling.

Example: You are writing a romance novel so you introduce the two lovers, as well as any other important characters to the reader. You will also take the time to provide insight as to where the book is taking place. This is where you can introduce the stakes as well, which essentially means you are telling the reader what is at stake and why it is important to the protagonist.

Step Two: The First Major Plot Point

The second step is to introduce the first major plot point to your reader. This should be defined by an event that takes place which forces the character to take action. You want this first major plot point to be considered the last scene in the first act so that readers are left wanting more. This is the finale of the first part of your book, so you want to leave it with some form of small cliffhanger. This both rewards the reader for reading by giving them some action to pay attention to, but also has them wondering what is going to come next as a result of the character's actions.

Example: The female character in your romance novel is walking home when an attacker tries to hurt her. The male character comes seemingly from nowhere and defends her honor, ensuring that she was protected and was not harmed by the attacker.

Step Three: First Half of Second Act

This is the part of the book where your character is coming back from the action they took at the end of the first act. Here you further explain what happened as a result of that plot point, as well as how your characters are dealing with it.

Example: As a result of him being the first to hit the attacker, despite him attempting to defend the female, the male role in your novel is being subjected to a criminal investigation. Because of this, he is trying to keep a low profile and avoid any further complications. The female is angry with the male for not calling the cops instead and allowing them to deal with it. She is upset that he has subjected himself to the criminal investigation through his actions, regardless of his reasoning.

Step Four: Second Major Plot Point

This is a plot point within' the story where the character who was attempting to regain their bearings from the first major plot point is forced back into action. Here, you want to work together with what said character has at stake to help the reader understand why they have been forced into action. Often the action is forced unto the character in the form of an ultimatum.

Example: Despite keeping a low profile for some time, the attacker returns and attempts to strike again. Only this time, he knows that the male is with the female and the attacker is attempting to force the male to act. He wants to have the male punished for attacking him, regardless of the fact that he was only attempting to protect her from the attacker. As a result, the male role is forced to decide between protecting her again or being faced with serious jail time. For the sake of these examples, let's say that he chooses to defend her honor once again.

Step Five: Second Half of Second Act

This is the part where all of the characters in the story begin to come into their own. Here, they are all grouping together to come against the antagonist. They are ensuring that the initial character is no longer left to take action on his or her own, but rather that they are supported by the other characters within' the story.

Example: This time, the female character is aware of what is going on and she is fighting to protect the male character. She is no longer angry with him for making the choice he made originally, and she is more willing to testify in his defense. They work together to get the attacker in trouble and to protect the male character through pleading that he was only practicing self-defense.

Step Six: Third Major Plot Point

This is where the protagonist's behavior appears to have led him or her to a place of defeat. In this part of the story, you want to introduce the idea that there may be no hope for this character and that they may be doomed because of the antagonistic forces. Here, they are beginning to feel as though they have hit rock bottom.

Example: Despite the female character testifying to the male character and fighting in his corner this time around, the court orders him guilty for assault. It appears that even though he was attempting to protect himself and the female character, no one is willing to see that. It seems there is no hope for him to avoid criminal charges altogether.

Step Seven: Third Act

In the third act, the protagonist is fighting against the antagonistic force as a last effort to take them down. Here they may not have total confidence that they can do it but they are not willing to give up just yet.

Example: The male character chooses to appeal the court ruling. Together, he and the female work to create a plan where they will prove that he is innocent and the attacker is the one who is truly guilty.

Step Eight: Climax

This is where there is a final face-off between the protagonist and antagonist. This is the deciding moment that is responsible for determining whether the story will end in favor of the antagonist, or in favor of the protagonist.

Example: The male character and the attacker face off in court. This is the part of the story that will determine whether the male is ruled guilty and is no longer welcome to appeal the charges, or whether the judge will see that he is actually innocent and it is the attacker who should be facing charges. For the sake of the example, we will say that it ends with the attacker being charged and the male being let off.

Step Nine: Resolution

This is where any loose ends from the story. It will also give insight to how the characters react to the climax and where they end up afterward. This is the wind down where readers are given the opportunity to know "what's next" and is required to avoid you from ending your book in a cliff-hanger.

Example: The female character is ecstatic that the male character is let free and they decide that they never want to risk facing a life without the other so they choose to get married.

As you can see, developing a strong story structure is important. Hopefully, through the use of the examples, you were able to understand how the structure lent a hand towards generating suspense and giving the reader a reason to keep reading. Because of how the story was structured and when certain pieces of information were revealed, the individual reading the story once it was complete would be engaged and would thus stay committed to reading the entire story so that they could discover how it ended.

It is important that you pay attention to the book in three sections as outlined above, as well as that you have a major plot point in each part. Dividing your story into three sections ensures that each part focuses on a particular element of the story and avoids you from going back and forth or otherwise introducing elements that are later forgotten about because you are not clear and focused on what you are writing. Having a major plot point in each section ensures that each section is rich and your reader is engaged the entire time. This is ultimately the structure you need in order to draw your reader forward and keep them moving through the story until they reach the end.

Chapter 3: Developing Your Story

Now that you are aware of what it takes to design a strong story structure, you may be wondering how you can develop a story that will fit with the structure! If you already have a general idea, then you can use the information from this section to help you strengthen that idea and ensure that all areas of your story are considered before them being structured and then written. If you have no idea as to what your story is going to be yet, use this chapter to help you identify a story and develop it so that it provides you with plenty of material to write your book about.

Study Existing Plots

When you are working towards developing your story one of the best ways to go about it is to read. Reading other people's stories gives you the opportunity to see what worked and what didn't, and it also provides you with inspiration to enrich your own story. While you don't want to be plagiarizing or stealing stories from other people, getting inspiration to enrich your own and strengthen the plot is always a great idea. This ensures that you are going to have a really strong story that provides enough material to engage your audience and keep them captive for the duration of the book.

When you are studying other people's stories you want to do more than just read them. You want to pay attention to who the characters are, how they develop throughout the novel, how the events take place including when and where, and all locations that the story takes place in. You should also identify the sequence that the locations are used in. Knowing more about these primary areas of the story allows you to get an idea of how books are written and what authors do in order to develop their own storyline. You can see the techniques in action and understand how they contribute to the overall experience being delivered in the story.

Draft Up Your Plot

When you are designing your plot there are some strategies you can use to see your plot come together without writing out the entire story first. The best way to do this is through drafting up your plot. You can do this by writing a paragraph or two from each ideal chapter and then read them in order. While it will obviously be missing many details, doing this will give you an idea of how the plot points flow together and if they are strong enough to give you plenty of writing material to work with.

Using a plotting strategy like this gives you the opportunity to look at your plot as a whole and make sure that it works effectively in the story you are writing. This helps you see what areas of the plot are rich and which aren't. You can also finalize the main plot sequencing and points before starting the writing process so that you are certain that it is in the order that you want and that it all works well together. This essentially gives you a birds-eye view of what your structure is and lets you know whether or not it works.

Create a Timeline

A great way to build your story is to create a timeline. This timeline should include all of the major plot points in chronological order. Seeing these together helps you identify how each one builds into the next one and makes sure that they work well together. If anything is missing or you feel there is a plot point that does not fit well in the overall story, then you can use this as an opportunity to eliminate it.

Similar to drafting your plot, creating a timeline allows you to take a birds-eye view at the work you have created and determine whether or not it works. The more you pay attention to the structure of your story from different elements now, the more you can be certain that it will work and produce a strong story in the long run.

Plan Character Development Along the Plot Line

After you have generated your plot draft and your timeline, take your characters into consideration. Pay attention to how you want them to develop along the storyline. It is natural for characters to change throughout stories, and even necessary in order for the story to progress. A great way to plan their development is to plan it alongside the story development. How is the development of the story going to contribute to the growth of the character? Consider this while you are deciding how your character will develop along the way.

Change the 5 "W's

A great way to ensure that you have developed the story strong enough is to check that you have changed the five w's along the way. The who, what, when, where, and why of the story should all develop or completely change along the progression of your story. In real life, these change from moment to moment and day to day. If you want your story to be realistic and relatable, you need to ensure that they are changed in your story as well.

If you want to take your story from good to great, these answers should not be simple and direct. Each one should have a series of answers that guide the element from the start of the book to the end. They should change in a way that convinces the reader that the change was natural and realistic, and helps the character feel as though it is a true story being told. Think back to your own day, for example you may have woken up in your home and now you are sitting in a coffee shop reading this book. You may have woken in a bad mood and now you are in a better one, or vice versa. The reasons as to why your mood change are also important to the story of your day. Who was involved in your day and what helped you pass the day by will have also changed from moment to moment. Just like your day naturally progressed as a story of its own, you need your story to progress in the same way. This ensures that your book goes in-depth enough to make it convincing to your reader. If any of the five w's are not developed enough, look for opportunities to strengthen them so that your story will be rich and full of realistic details.

Design a Story Board

Creating a storyboard is another great way to look at the structure of your story. A great way to create the storyboard is to write each major plot point and important element on a cue card or post it so that they can easily be moved around to create the final story map. This gives you a great opportunity to see how each event works together and organize them effortlessly without having to scratch out things and replace them everywhere.

Consider Subplots

Creating subplots that fit in seamlessly with your overall story is a great way to enrich the story experience and add more depth to it while also encouraging reader engagement. Subplots are essentially the "what else" part of the story. For example, if you are writing a book about the main character who is seeking justice, consider including elements of why this justice is so important for this character. Perhaps they want the criminal incarcerated because he or she deserves to be, but it may also be because the protagonist has allowed others to walk all over him for too long and he is ready to stand up for himself. Therefore, getting justice is both about having justice served *and* about building the confidence to actually fight for what is right.

Subplots are an incredible story developing strategy that can help you create a story that is much richer in context. You can include as many or as few subplots as you want, but make sure that each one makes sense to the overall story itself. They should work together with the main plot, rather than going against it or straying away from it completely.

Incorporate Driven Elements

All of the best stories incorporate one specific element that enables the story to be so great. That is the element of change. In order to create change, there are two very specific things you need. Character-driven and action-driven elements to your story. These elements are two things that can help incorporate change into your story in such a way that yours fosters all of the greatness that all of the other best titles do.

The reason why change is so powerful in a story is that that is what drives the story forward. People are curious to know about how characters change and grow throughout the course of the story every bit as much as they are interested in learning about how the story develops itself. People do not want to read a story about static characters who do the same thing every day and nothing changes. That would be extremely boring and would lead to them closing the book and turning away from it entirely. Think about it, would you read a book like that? Likewise, people are not interested in a book that has minimal change, or where the change only occurs on one very specific thing. Instead, people want to see the entire story change. They want to see the characters grow, they want to see the circumstances evolve, and they want to see the protagonist, and even the antagonist, end up somewhere completely different from where they were when the story changed. Incorporating as much natural and realistic change as possible helps drive your story forward and keep it both interesting and engaging.

As previously mentioned, there are two different types of change you can use to drive your story forward: character-driven change, and action-driven change. Both of these elements should be included in your own story if you want a diverse and realistic story that will help keep your readers engaged and reading your book all the way until the last page.

Character-driven change is used by showing the stakes the character has. For example, their child, their family, their significant other, their career. By incorporating these stakes and giving the reader insight as to why they are so important to the character, you can use them as an opportunity to drive the story forward. The most important thing to understand is that without character-driven change, there is no story. Character-driven change is essentially the answer to "why" your character is doing anything that takes place in the story. This explains why they will do almost anything, even stuff that seems highly irrational or nonsensical, in various situations. "Because my child is sick" or, "because I could lose my job" for example, would be the stakes and therefore would answer "why" the character is so invested in something. By creating this type of explanation and therefore emotional attachment from the reader to the character, and furthermore the character's stakes, you can make virtually every part of the story that much more engaging and interesting for your reader. Without character-driven change, your readers are not given an opportunity to understand why they need to care about the events taking place in your book.

Action-driven change is an entirely different form of change. This is the change whereby specific actions happen that cause the story to drive forward. High-speed chases, break-ins, getting arrested, being put on the chopping block at work, the spouse falling in love with someone else, the kid getting into trouble, all of these would constitute as action-drive changes. For the most part, these are actions that are taking place that cannot be stopped or influenced by your protagonist. Instead, the protagonist must find a way to respond and react to these actions.

When you use character-driven change effectively, action-driven change becomes that much more intriguing and engaging for your reader. Because they understand the stakes and have developed an emotional attachment to your characters, they are much more concerned with the action, as well as the outcome. It is important that you use a balanced amount of both types of changes in your story. This will help you round out your story and keep it moving forward without being too heavily charged in one direction or another. Furthermore, you want to make sure that you don't go overboard on the change. While it does drive the story forward, you want to make sure that you use it in a very realistic and natural manner. This helps the reader relate to the story and believe it, instead of feeling as though it is completely unlikely and therefore it is not relatable. If a reader cannot relate to a story in one way or another, they are not going to continue reading it because it will be too unbelievable for them.

Question Yourself

When you are in the process of developing your story, make sure you question yourself a lot along the way. The more you question yourself, your intentions, the story and the plot line, the more you can develop it. Questioning it ultimately gives you the opportunity to see where any loopholes may lie, if any part of the plot is weak, or if there is any reason that you should need to develop part of the story more. It also helps you identify where there may be too much action or development going on so that you can scale it back. If you are not taking the time to question yourself and your story structure, you may be missing important things that could take away from the value of your story altogether.

Some great questions to ask yourself include ones such as:

- Why has the character changed, how did the change happen, and what was the purpose of this change?

- How much has the character changed since the beginning of the story?

- Is the change natural and believable?

- What has each plot point taught the characters, thus teaching them about the story's primary situation or conflict?

- Can you identify some core themes within' the story? Are there too many or too few core themes taking place?

- Is the story believable? Does it flow naturally?

- Does the story move forward effectively, or is it too slow?

Asking yourself these questions will help ensure that each part of your story structure is strong and that it will help you produce a believable, relatable, and enjoyable story that is interesting and engaging. If you find that your answer is "no" or "I don't know" to any of the questions above, take the time to further explore that question and find ways that you can strengthen the story structure itself.

Get Feedback

Finally, it is important that you take the time to get feedback on your story structure. As with most things, having someone else take a look and give you some insight as to where the strengths and weaknesses lie and if any adaptations or alterations should be made means that nothing will be missed. This is the best way to make sure that you have a strong structure going into your story that will both serve you and serve your readers by giving you enough material and answers to generate an interesting an engaging story.

If you do not personally know someone who can provide you with feedback, there are many online platforms and forums that you can turn to where you can find someone to help you with looking over the structure. Furthermore, you can also look to find someone from your ideal target audience and have them look over the structure for you. Regardless of who you get to help you with the structure, do your best to make sure it is someone who is either in or thoroughly understands your target audience, and ideally someone with some experience in story structure. Having someone who intimately knows you are trying to reach and what you are trying to say can help significantly as it ensures that any feedback or critique they provide you with is accurate and helpful. Those who are unclear on the audience you are trying to reach or who have zero understanding of story structure or what is required in order to make a good book may not be able to provide you with information that will help you improve your structure. In fact, they may even have you questioning parts that you should not need to question. It is important that the person you choose to work with understands your needs.

Chapter 4: Creating Suspense

Regardless of what genre you are writing for, you need to be skilled in creating suspense for your story. Suspense is the element that keeps readers wondering what is coming next and how events are going to unfold. When used properly, suspense can be what draws one plot point to the next. If you want to create a compelling and convincing fiction novel that encourages readers to continue reading, you are going to need to master the art of creating suspense. The next ten tips are about how you can begin creating suspense in your own novel to keep your readers wanting more.

Understand Your Genre

Before you begin creating suspense, it is important that you understand the genre you are writing in. Each genre uses suspense differently to draw characters forward and keep readers coming back. If you want to do your book justice, you need to practice using suspense for your unique genre.

Let's take a look at three different types of novels and where the suspense would come into play for each type.

Mystery: A horror or major event takes place in the first chapter and the rest of the book is spent figuring out why the event occurred and who was responsible for it. For example, the protagonist's spouse was killed in the first chapter and the rest of the book is spent uncovering who was responsible.

Romance: You build up to the point where the two lovers finally get together. The climax, or the two getting together, officially takes place later in the book, usually within' the last couple of chapters. For example, two lovers know they're meant to be together but the timing never seems right. One is always dating someone else when the other is available for the relationship to work. As a result, they are never able to get together until the end when they finally make it work.

Suspense: The knowledge of an impending horror is upon the characters in the novel and they spend the entire time trying to avoid it until they can no longer keep it from happening. For example, someone knows they are going to jail for embezzlement but doesn't know when. This character knows that he has been tracked and that the FBI is well aware of what has been going on. He does not know when he will be taken down, but it will happen.

Provide Adequate Viewpoints

When it comes to developing a strong case of suspense in your novel, you need to give the reader adequate knowledge. This comes from providing them with different viewpoints. Through this, you can give them insight to the protagonist's side of things, and the antagonist's side of things. The best way to get a lot of suspense building in your book is by giving your reader insight as to what is going to happen before the protagonist knows. This gives the writer the opportunity to increase the emotional attachment to the protagonist and the stakes. The reader is drawn along an experience where they know what is yet to come but they have to watch the protagonist find out and learn the consequences of certain actions. The tension that builds on the reader because of what they know that the protagonist doesn't know is similar to someone who has a secret they're not allowed to tell. It engages the reader and makes them want to know more and to understand where the book will end up.

Put Time on Your Side

Time is an incredible tool when it comes to writing a book with suspense. You want to use time on your side so that you can increase the amount of suspense in the novel. Time gives you the opportunity to make the reader feel as though the protagonist is working against the clock. Everything they are doing should have some form of time constraint on it. Ideally, it should appear as though the clock is working in favor of the antagonist or antagonistic force to keep the suspense strong. For example, if you were writing a mystery novel about a murder that took place, it should seem as though the protagonist doesn't have enough time to find the murderer. Perhaps there is some jurisdiction law that states that if the person is not found within' a set amount of time the charges won't be as strong, or the murderer has been leaving clues that they have left town and it gets harder and harder to find who they are. Several dead end leads are exhausted before the protagonist finally discovers who the murderer was in the end. Putting time on your side lets you build suspense by creating the illusion that something won't happen, even though it needs to.

Keep The Stakes High

The stakes that you use in a story should be high enough to justify a high amount of suspense. The higher the stakes the more pressing the need to protect them is, both in the mind of the character and the reader. While you don't need to choose devastating stakes that are excessively high, picking ones that someone would actually be desperate to protect will ensure that your reader understands why the protagonist is so passionate about protecting their stakes. Some examples would include an executive who is facing being exposed for shady business dealings, therefore costing them their job and their reputation and making them unlikeable for other employers. Or, perhaps a male is in love with a female in a romance novel, but he grows tired of waiting for her to make up her mind so he pursues a relationship with someone else. She realizes she wants him more than anything but must figure out a way to tell him, and fast, before he marries the other person or realizes that he does not want to be with her altogether. Alternatively, you may choose to write a story about someone with a powerful societal position being murdered and they must find out who did it before they strike another powerful member of society. By keeping the stakes high but reasonable, you make it very clear as to why your reader needs to be so concerned with what is taking place in the book. The stronger your stakes are, the more your reader will be passionate alongside your character to ensure that they are not lost.

Don't Be Afraid to Apply Pressure

Pressure is a great way to add suspense to any novel. The odds should be stacked well against your character and it should take a great amount of effort and energy for them to tip the odds in their favor and save the day. The more the odds are stacked against them, the higher the pressure is and therefore the more you can draw the reader to wondering if they will ever be able to beat the odds. When they finally do, the reader and character alike will feel a great deal of relief from the experience.

When you are writing about creating pressure, make sure that you never lead your protagonist right to the breaking point. They should bend and cripple under pressure, but they should never stop pushing. You should ensure that they are always pushed *almost* too far so that they have *just* enough amount of energy to push back and it is at that time that they finally beat the antagonistic force and experience success in their heroic attempts.

Make Use of Dilemmas

Dilemmas are a great way to increase suspense in a story and have your reader highly engaged. Dilemmas present a "this or that" action for the character. They should be forced into action, and make sure that the pressure is on for it to happen fast. When dilemmas are being thrown towards your character it is important to make sure that they are being thrown by the antagonist most often. This should present the idea that the protagonist cannot win in the situation. For example, for them to save one character another must die, they can either lose their family and save their job or lose their job and save their family, or even indulging in alcohol after swearing to sobriety at some point within' the novel.

When you are presenting dilemmas, make sure that the antagonist always crosses the line. Because they are the villain, they shouldn't even think twice about going across it. However, the protagonist should always be forced with their morals and values. Should they do one, or the other? Which will be the less of two evils? Is there a way that they can make the best of both horrible situations? True to heroic nature, they should be struggling to find the answer to the dilemma.

One great reason why dilemmas work is because you can apply pressure and time constraints so that the protagonist is forced to make a decision fast, which puts pressure on him and gets the reader worried about what is going to happen. Using these three strategies together is a great way to build suspense throughout your book.

Complicate Things

You don't need to restrict to just presenting your protagonist with one or even two conflicts at any given time. Instead, feel free to pile on the complications every now and again. The more complicated things get, the more difficult it will be for them to come up with the solution and make the right choice. At times, it should feel like the protagonist is trying to juggle several balls at once and he is just barely keeping them from dropping every time. This is a great time to push the protagonist almost to the point of breaking before bringing them back in for a final and much awaited victory.

Avoid Becoming Predictable

When your book runs too smoothly, it becomes predictable. It also becomes uninteresting and the readers struggle to relate to it. Life is not about being smooth and predictable. Most often we are all living in a hot mess where we are balancing many different things and trying to stay afloat along the way. If you want to write a great book, it should be similar to this. Throw random curveballs in, take a spin somewhere where one wasn't expected, and have your reader surprised at some of the elements that are being tossed in, and when. When it comes to writing, don't let the hero rely on the idea that everything will go in their favor. In fact, almost nothing should. This way when it finally does, it will come as a surprise. Furthermore, your antagonist shouldn't go with everything going in their way, either. Let both of them face challenges, twists and turns along the way. The more they are affected by curveballs and unexpected experiences, the more realistic the story will be. Make the protagonist slip up and result in an almost-victory instead of a true victory, and let the antagonist fail at the most inconvenient of times for them. This keeps your readers on their toes and unsure about what is going to happen, when.

Develop Your Villain

Your villain is the antagonistic force in your book, and they need to be developed really well. Your reader should be mentally pushing against the villain, and rooting for the hero. As a result, you need to have a really well developed villain that has the reader truly believing and feeling as though they are a nasty force to be reckoned with.

Make sure that you use the right villain for your novel genre, as well. In a mystery, for example, it should not be clear as to who the villain is until the end. With a romance novel on the other hand, the villain might be time itself, or the person coming between the two lovers and keeping them apart. Alternatively, in a suspense novel the villain should be highly visible at all times and people should ultimately just be wondering when they will finally strike. The more you understand what type of villain is appropriate for your unique genre, the easier it will be to create one that is believable and extremely well developed.

When you develop your antagonist, make sure that you are very specific on who they are and what makes them tick. You want this character to be so developed that your reader feels as though they personally know them. Furthermore, your antagonist should change throughout the story, which is easiest to prove if your reader knows who they are from how you've written about them.

Develop Your Hero

In addition to developing your villain, you need to develop your hero. This is the one that finally defeats the antagonistic force and creates the victory of the story. The best way to create a strong hero is to really build on the character and give the reader plenty of reasons to love them. This is the character your reader is going to follow throughout the story. This is who they will be rooting for, worrying for, and curious about. They want to know everything they can about this character, and they have mentally prepared themselves to be on their side emotionally. Therefore, you need to use this character to not only build an emotional attachment between your reader and your protagonist, but also to use that attachment to manipulate the emotions of your reader. The protagonist is the character that you are going to leverage in order to get your reader nervous, curious, excited, happy, sad, angry, and any other emotion you want them to engage in throughout the experience. The best way to do that is to have a well-developed character that your reader can truly feel as though they have befriended.

Chapter 5: Additional Story Structure Tips

In addition to tips on basic story structure, developing a strong story, and how to create suspense, there are many other great tips that can help you when it comes to story structures. Now that you have the three important elements down, you can explore additional tips that will take you further into the realm of pro writer and help you generate a story that is going to be fantastic. The following tips are provided from real authors who have experience in writing their own high quality fiction materials. By following these tips, you can ensure that you don't only have a great story structure, but a phenomenal one.

Research Different Story Structures

Although there is a basic system that virtually all structures follow, it is important to understand that there are many modifications and alterations made to this structure in true writing. After all, if every story followed the basic structure down to the last detail then there would be no point in reading. We would be able to read the first chapter and know exactly how a book was going to turn out. By making modifications to the structure and playing it around in different ways, writers have the ability to stick to a structure that works while also providing a script that is unique, unpredictable, and engaging for readers.

Armed with this knowledge, you can prepare yourself to start researching many different story structures. The best way is to read other people's novels and do your best to identify the structure within' them. As you are reading, write down the major plot points and other key details that come into play with these plot points. Doing this will help you identify a series of structures that are used to create incredible novels, and how the writers spun them to work for the story. Do this several times over and pay attention to patterns that arise. Then, choose the structure you like most and make it work for your novel!

Stick to Structures that Are Traditional for Your Genre

For the best results, it is important that you stick to structures that are traditional to your genre. Although this may sound like a surefire way to create a story that sounds like every other story in the genre, it actually isn't. You will learn more about why in a moment. In the meantime, it is important that you understand why it is a good idea to stick to these traditional structures.

Each structure is designed to create a different effect for the story. Some build suspense, some build mystery, and some build both. Depending on what genre you are writing for, you are going to want to go for a structure that provides you with the right elements of virtually everything. These are going to be elements of suspense, story building opportunities, character development opportunities, and more. Each genre tends to be told in a unique way because it achieves a specific result. Therefore, each structure that is unique to each genre is built to help achieve that specific result. For example, you wouldn't want to use a suspense structure for a mystery novel because you would thus be identifying the perpetrator immediately. Likewise, you wouldn't want to use a mystery structure in a suspense novel because it would destroy the element of suspense by not giving enough information to the reader.

It is important that you do not reinvent the wheel, but rather you explore the different styles of wheels that exist for your market. Furthermore, just because you are limited to only using structures that are traditional for your genre does not mean that there is only one single structure you can follow. Each genre has its own selection of structures that will and won't work. The best way to identify which one you want to use is to read them, as described in the previous section, and pay attention to each type of structure you come across. As you do, identify which one would work best for your unique story and enlist that as your structure of choice.

Structure the Novel to Your Central Theme

As you are designing the structure for your novel, make sure that you are conforming the structure to fit the central theme of your novel and not the other way around. You never want to be derailing or detracting from the story as an attempt to stick to your structure. Remember, a structure is supposed to be a guideline that gets you to where you need to go. You do not have to follow it down to every last detail in order for your story to be a good one. Instead, you want to pay attention to the story structure and write your novel with that structure in mind.

Stories that are written to strictly to the guidelines set out in the structure end up sounding very forced and uncomfortable. Readers will often lose engagement quickly because the story becomes predictable and unnatural. They cannot relate to the story so they do not want to read it any longer. Ultimately, it takes away from the reader's experiences and kills the chance of your novel being greater.

To elaborate on how the structure *should* be used, we will explore how exactly you can enforce its guidelines. One of the biggest things you want to pay attention to, and use your structure for, is to ensure that your book stays focused on the central theme. If your novel strays too far away from the central theme at any given point, it may take away from the story overall. You never want to over share or get off track on a topic that does not contribute to the central theme or purpose of your novel. This is where your story structure comes in handy. Having a structure that can help keep you on track is highly valuable as it ensures that you do not derail your story and end up with a novel about love that gets too off track and ends up being about one person's career, or something else. Essentially you want to employ your story structure as a guide to keep you on track and to build a strong story, but you do not want to follow it so closely that you snuff out the quality of your story and produce something generic and predictable.

Modify the Template to Suit Your Plot

To expand further on the previous tip, it is important to work on modifying your template to suit your plot. Although you do not want to create an entirely new structure for your novel, or take one from the wrong genre, this does not mean that you cannot modify the template. For example, if you would prefer a certain plot point to happen sooner rather than later, or vice versa, you certainly have creative freedom to make this decision. Remember, you are a storyteller and your story is your work of art. Just because there are certain methods to use doesn't mean you can't get creative. For example, paint brushes are what you are *supposed* to paint with, but many choose to paint with sponges or even rags instead. Some even use a different material altogether, and yet the art is still incredible beautiful. In fact, it may be even more beautiful because of the unique method used. In this analogy, a different approach was used but the same bare basic structure was used: a tool was used to pick up paint and apply it to a canvas. You can easily modify certain parts of that, such as by changing your tools or picking a unique canvas, but at the very root is the same structure. The same goes for writing.

Just because authors before you have always used a specific template doesn't mean you cannot modify that template to suit your story. If you find that certain elements would serve better at a different area in the story, you are always welcome to do that. The best thing you can do as a writer is exercise your creative freedom. When you let loose from expectations and open yourself up to generate phenomenal content, inevitably you generate phenomenal content. As long as you stick to the bare bones basics with your structure, you are going to end up with a great story. If on the off chance you don't, it is a great opportunity to further research the structure and understand where you went wrong and how you could create a better story and structure in the future.

Create the Structure First, Modify it Later

It is always a good idea to begin your story with a strong structure. That being said, you should seek to create the structure before you begin writing. Having your structure created first and then creating a story around that structure helps ensure that you are staying on track with the basics. However, that does not mean that you are restricted to only writing to that specific structure.

As writers carry along the process of writing, they often find that it takes them down a natural path and therefore certain elements of their original structure no longer serve the story as powerfully as they could. The best thing to do in this circumstances is to reevaluate the structure and modify it so that it better suits the story in the direction that you have taken it. When you do this, you open yourself up to the opportunity of creating something much more powerful than you originally set out to do.

Creating a story is not always as straightforward as it seems. In many cases you will go into it with a very specific idea of what you want the story to be like and as a result of your writing process you discover that it actually works for reasons other than you thought so it naturally evolves away from your initial intentions. The best thing you can do in these circumstances is honor that natural evolution in your story and work with it. If you try and go against it in order to stick to your original structure you may end up creating a strange and unnatural twist backward, or it will otherwise not flow well. In order to give yourself creative freedom while also holding on to some sense of direction, the best thing to do is to start with a structure and modify it if your story evolves away from the initial structure you laid out for it. This will keep you on track while also giving you the potential to create an incredible story.

Hide the Structure in Your Writing

When it comes to the writing process, you want to ensure that you are hiding the structure within' your writing. It should not be painfully obvious what structure you have used. If it is, then your story will become predictable and people will lose interest. Virtually every story structure has been used several times over. This means that people will have a pretty easy ability to link your strategies together and determine what the novel will end like regardless of whether or not they have read it. They will also likely discover what major plot points are going to occur well before they ever happen. When the book becomes this predictable, it also becomes highly uninteresting.

A great writer knows how to hide the structure within' the story. Make things happen sooner or later than expected, twist away from the structure here and there to blend it in, and do your best to avoid going very clearly from point one to point two. You want your readers to question what is happening and be surprised along the way. Give them the idea that they have already arrived at the major plot point with one activity and then blow them out of the water with something much bigger. Keep the element of surprise active and use it as your weapon to bury the structure. The less obvious your structure is, the more unpredictable your story becomes and therefore the more power you have as the author to keep your reader engaged and have them wanting to learn more about what you have yet to tell them.

Keep Your Structure Organized and Handy

For a practical writing tip in regards to your structure, it is important that you keep it organized and that it is available at all times when you are writing. Your structure will prove to be a highly valuable tool when it comes to producing your novel. Being able to refer back to it at different points and identify where you are at will help you know where to go with your story, as well as help you stay focused on the central theme and overall purpose of your book.

A great way to keep your structure handy and useful during the writing process is to have it written down somewhere, such as on cue cards, and nearby whenever you are writing. This way you can identify where you have already been on the structure and where you have yet to go. It will also provide you with the ability to refer back to it regularly, as well as effortlessly revise it as needed. The reason why you might want to make your "final" structure on cue cards is because if you choose to modify it along the way you can easily do it without having to completely start over or rewrite it. This makes it effortless for you to modify it as needed and keep the parts you want.

Experiment

There is nothing more valuable than hands-on practice when it comes to any hobby, and this fact is not lost on writing. If you are looking for an opportunity to create an incredible book, take any chance you have to experiment. There are many ways that you can experiment when it comes to writing, and each can help you increase your understanding of story structures and how they work into the overall book, as well as how you can use your unique writing style to make the most of your story structure.

One great method is to take note of a few different story structures that will work effectively for the genre you are writing in and then draft your story out based on these. This means that you want to write a few paragraphs on each part of the structure and then read them together. It will give you the opportunity to see how your story would work together and if you have generated a strong enough story structure for your book. Another method is to practice writing short stories with different structures in a smaller way. While you won't be able to pack as much into the story as you would with a novel, it will give you a better idea of how your novel would sound with each unique structure in place.

Experimentation is the best way to practice writing and get an idea for what you like and what you don't like. If you are serious about it and you have time, practicing writing each novel with different structures and employing different strategies is a great way to see each structure in action and get a feel for how it works for your books. You can identify how the structure serves your story and where it might be weak, as well as how you can embed the structure within' the story using unique writing strategies to hide it from plain sight. This is a great way to practice writing overall and increase your skill if you are interested and have the time to invest.

Take Notes

Finally, a great method to use when it comes to learning and growing as a writer or as virtually anything is to take notes. When you are reading other books, take notes on what you like and don't like about the book, particularly when it comes to the structure of the book. When you are writing your own books, pay attention to where you have struggled and where you are succeeding. On the points where you a struggling, explore ways that you could make it easier. When it comes to each unique structure, write down how it serves your story and any thoughts you might have about how it could be better next time, or when you go through the editing process.

Taking notes allows you to review what you have already thought and felt about certain experiences with your story and its structure and gives you something easy and finite to look back on. When you take notes it means that you are not going to forget about or lose your thoughts in the process. This means that you can hold onto them and make the necessary changes without having to attempt to remember what it was that you wanted to do in the first place.

There are many great strategies you can use to strengthen your story structure immediately, as well as to help you increase your skills and become a better story writer through your structure over time. The more you emphasize on learning this skill now, the greater you will be at is as you go on. Remember that a strong structure can truly make or break a story. A bad structure equals a bad story, a good one equals a good story and a great structure will return you a great story. If you want to be great, you have to practice being great from the start. Over time and with practice you will graduate from being great to being phenomenal!

Conclusion

Thank you for reading *"Story Structure: Step-by-Step | Essential Story Building, Story Development and Suspense Writing Tricks Any Writer Can Learn"*. This book was designed to assist you in learning everything you need to know about story structures, including how you can make an incredible one.

I hope this book was able to elaborate on the concept of story structures, including what they are and why they are important. I also hope that you were able to learn plenty about how you can create your own story structure, develop your story, create suspense, and ultimately strengthen the structure of your story in order to create a phenomenal book.

The next step is to build your story structure and use it alongside the creation of your new book. Take your time and follow the steps within' this book to ensure that you have a strong structure that will serve you in the process of creating your book. Remember, as you go about the writing process you will want to check back to your structure to ensure that you are sticking to your original plan. However, if you find that your structure is no longer serving the overall creation of your story, you can always modify your structure for stronger impact. Sometimes the writing process can alter our plans and take us down a separate natural path. If this happens, ensure that you use the structure to support your story and the other way around.

Thank you!

More by Sandy Marsh

Discover all books from the Writing Best Seller Series by Sandy Marsh at:

bit.ly/sandy-marsh

Book 1: *How to Write a Novel*

Book 2: *Outlining*

Book 3: *Story Structure*

Book 4: *Plotting*

Book 5: *Character Development*

Book 6: *How to Write a Screenplay*

Themed book bundles available at discounted prices:

bit.ly/sandy-marsh